D1537249

THE
CROSS

Register This New Book

Benefits of Registering*

- ✓ FREE **replacements** of lost or damaged books

- ✓ FREE **audiobook** – *Pilgrim's Progress,* audiobook edition

- ✓ FREE information about new titles and other **freebies**

www.anekopress.com/new-book-registration

*See our website for requirements and limitations.

THE CROSS

Crucified with Christ, and Christ Alive in Me

J. C. RYLE

We love hearing from our readers. Please contact us at www.anekopress.com/questions-comments with any questions, comments, or suggestions.

The Cross – J. C. Ryle

Revised Edition Copyright © 2019

First edition published 1852

Scripture quotations are taken from the Jubilee Bible, copyright © 2000, 2001, 2010, 2013 by Russell M. Stendal. Used by permission of Russell M. Stendal, Bogota, Colombia. All rights reserved.

Cover Design: Jonathan Lewis

Editors: Sheila Wilkinson and Ruth Clark

Printed in Hong Kong

Aneko Press

www.anekopress.com

Aneko Press, Life Sentence Publishing, and our logos are trademarks of

Life Sentence Publishing, Inc.
203 E. Birch Street
P.O. Box 652
Abbotsford, WI 54405

RELIGION / Christian Theology / Soteriology

Paperback ISBN: 978-1-62245-641-3

eBook ISBN: 978-1-62245-642-0

10   9   8   7   6   5   4   3

Available where books are sold

Contents

Introduction ix

Ch. 1: What the Apostle Paul Did Not Glory In 1

Ch. 2: What to Understand about the Cross of
Christ – What Paul Gloried In 9

Ch. 3: Why All Christians Should Glory in the Cross
of Christ 17

J. C. Ryle – A Brief Biography 37

Other Similar Titles 43

In no wise should I glory, except in the cross of our Lord Jesus Christ. – Galatians 6:14

Introduction

What do you think and feel about the cross of Christ? You live in a Christian land. You probably attend the worship of a Christian church. You have perhaps been baptized in the name of Christ. You profess and call yourself a Christian. All this is well; it is more than can be said of millions in the world. But all this is no answer to my question, "What do you think and feel about the cross of Christ?"

I want to tell you what the greatest Christian who ever lived thought of the cross of Christ. He has written down his opinion and given his judgment in words that cannot be mistaken. The man I refer to is the apostle Paul. You will find his words in the letter which the Holy Spirit inspired him to write to the Galatians; the words in which his judgment is set down are these: *in no wise should I glory, except in the cross of our Lord Jesus Christ* (Galatians 6:14).

Now what did Paul mean by this? He meant to declare strongly that he trusted in nothing but Jesus Christ crucified for the pardon of his sins and the salvation of his soul. Let others, if they would, look elsewhere for salvation; let others, if they were so disposed, trust in other things for pardon and peace. But for his part, the apostle was determined to rest on nothing, lean on nothing, build his hope on nothing, place confidence in nothing, and glory in nothing except *the cross of our Lord Jesus Christ.*

Reader, let me talk to you about this subject. Believe me, it is one of deepest importance. This is no mere question of controversy; this is not one of those points on which men may agree to differ and feel that differences will not shut them out of heaven. A man must be right on this subject, or he is lost forever. Heaven or hell, happiness or misery, life or death, blessing or cursing in the last day – all hinges on the answer to this question: "What do you think about the cross of Christ?" Let me show you:

1. What the apostle Paul did not glory in

2. What Paul gloried in

3. Why all Christians should think and feel about the cross like Paul

What the Apostle Paul Did Not Glory In

The apostle Paul might have gloried in many things, if he had thought as some do today. If ever there was a person on earth who had something to boast of, that man was the great apostle of the Gentiles. If he did not dare to glory, who should?

He never gloried in his *national privileges*. He was a Jew by birth, as he tells us he was *an Hebrew of Hebrews* (Philippians 3:5). Like many of his brethren, he might have said, "I have Abraham for my forefather. I am not a dark, unenlightened heathen; I am one of the favored people of God: I have been admitted into covenant with God by circumcision. I am a far better man than the ignorant Gentiles." But he never said that but declared *those things which were gain to me, I counted loss for*

Christ (Philippians 3:7). He never gloried in anything of this kind. Never for one moment!

He never gloried in his *own works.* No one ever worked so hard for God as he did. He was more abundant in labors than any of the apostles (2 Corinthians 11:23). No living man ever preached so much, traveled so much, and endured so many hardships for Christ's cause. No one ever converted so many souls, did so much good to the world, and made himself so useful to mankind. No father of the early church, no reformer, no Puritan, no missionary, no minister, no layman – no one man could ever be named who did so many good works as the apostle Paul. But did he ever glory in them as if they were in the least meritorious and could save his soul? Never! Never for one moment!

He never gloried in his *knowledge.* He was a man of great natural gifts, and after he was converted, the Holy Spirit gave him even greater gifts. He was a mighty preacher, and a mighty speaker, and a mighty writer. He was as great with his pen as he was with his tongue. He could reason equally well with Jews and Gentiles. He could argue with infidels at Corinth, or Pharisees at Jerusalem, or the self-righteous people in Galatia. He knew many deep things. He had been in the third heaven and had heard unspeakable words (2 Corinthians 12:1-4). He had received the spirit of prophecy and could explain things yet to come. But did he ever glory in his knowledge as if it could justify him before God? Never! Never for one moment!

He never gloried in his *graces*. If ever there was one who abounded in graces, that man was Paul. He was full of love. How tenderly and affectionately he used to write. He could feel for souls like a mother or a nurse feeling for her child. He was a bold man. He cared not whom he opposed when truth was at stake. He cared not what risks he ran when souls could be won. He was a self-denying man – *in many watches, in hunger and thirst, in many fasts, in cold and naked-ness* (2 Corinthians 11:27). He was a humble man. He thought himself *less than the least of all saints* and the chief of sinners (Ephesians 3:8; 1 Timothy 1:15). He was a prayerful man. At the beginning of his epistles he expressed himself as a thankful man. His thanks-givings and his prayers walked side by side, but he never gloried in all this, never valued himself because of it, never rested his soul's hopes on it. Oh no, never for a moment!

He never gloried in his *churchmanship*. If ever there was a good churchman, that man was Paul. He was a chosen apostle. He was a founder of churches and an ordainer of ministers: Timothy, Titus, and many elders received their first commission from his hands. He began services in many dark places, observed the Lord's Supper, and held many meetings for prayer, and praise, and preaching. He set up the discipline in many young churches. Paul described qualifications for bishops and deacons and explained how to provide for widows and honor the elders (1 Timothy 3:1-5:25). But did he ever glory in his office and church standing? Does he ever speak as if his churchmanship would save him, justify him, remove his sins, and make him acceptable before God? Oh no, never! Never for a moment!

And now consider what I say. If the apostle Paul never gloried in any of these things, who in all the world, from one end to the other, has any right to glory in these qualities today? If Paul said, "God forbid that I should glory in anything except the cross," who should dare to say, "I have something to glory in; I am a better man than Paul"?

Who is there among the readers of this small book that trusts in any goodness of his own? Who is there that is resting on his own accomplishments, his own morality, or his own performances of any kind? Who is there that is placing the weight of his soul on anything of his own in the smallest possible degree?

Who is there among the readers of this book that trusts in his church membership for salvation? Who values himself on his baptism, his attendance at the

Lord's Table, his church attendance on Sundays, or his daily services during the week and says to himself, "What do I lack?" Learn today that you are not like Paul. Your Christianity is not the Christianity of the New Testament. Paul would not glory in anything but the cross. Neither should you.

Oh, beware of self-righteousness. Open sin kills thousands of souls. Self-righteousness kills tens of thousands. Go and study humility with the great apostle of the Gentiles. Go and sit with Paul at the foot of the cross. Give up your secret pride. Cast away your vain ideas of your own goodness. Be thankful if you have grace, but never glory in it for a moment. Work for God and Christ with heart and soul and mind and strength, but never dream for a second of placing confidence in any work of your own.

Think, you who take comfort in some fancied ideas of your own goodness; think, you who wrap yourselves up in the notion that all must be right if I stay in my church; think for a moment what a sandy foundation you are building! Think for a moment how miserably defective your hopes and pleas will look in the hour of death and in the day of judgment!

Whatever men may say of their own goodness while they are strong and healthy, they will find little to say of it when they are sick and dying. Whatever merit they may see in their own works here in this world, they discover no merit in them when they stand before the bar of Christ. The light of that great day of judgment will make a wonderful difference in the appearance of all their doings. It will strip off the tinsel, shrivel up the complexion, and expose the rottenness of many deeds that are now called good. Their wheat will prove to be nothing but chaff; their gold will be found to be nothing but dross. Millions of so-called good works will turn out to have been utterly defective and graceless. They were genuine and valued among men, but they will prove light and worthless in the balance of God. They will be found to have been like the whitened sepulchres of old, fair and beautiful outside but full of corruption within. Alas, for the man who can look forward to the day of judgment and place his soul in the smallest degree on anything of his own![1]

Once more I say, beware of self-righteousness in

---

1   "Howsoever men when they sit at ease, do vainly tickle their own hearts with the wanton conceit of I know not what proportionable correspondence between their merits and their rewards, which in the trance of their high speculations, they dream that God hath measured and laid up as it were in bundles for them; we see, notwithstanding, by daily experience, in a number even of them, that when the hour of death approacheth, when they secretly hear themselves summoned to appear and stand at the bar of that Judge, whose brightness causeth the eyes of angels themselves to dazzle, all those idle imaginations do then begin to hide their faces. To name merits then is to lay their souls upon the rack. The memory of their own deeds is loathsome unto them. They forsake all things wherein they have put any trust and confidence. No staff to lean upon, no rest, no ease, no comfort then, but only in Christ Jesus." – Richard Hooker, *Of the Laws of Ecclesiastical Policy*, 1586.

every possible shape and form. Some people receive as much harm from their fancied virtues as others do from their sins. Take heed, lest you be one. Rest not until your heart beats in tune with Paul's. Rest not until you can say with him, God forbid that I should glory in anything but the cross.

What to Understand about the Cross of Christ – What Paul Gloried In

The cross is an expression that is used with more than one meaning in the Bible. What did Paul mean when he said, *I glory in the cross of Christ* in the epistle to the Galatians? This is the point I wish to make clear.

The cross sometimes means that wooden cross on which the Lord Jesus was nailed and put to death on Mount Calvary. This is what Paul had in his mind's eye when he told the Philippians that Christ *became obedient unto death, even the death of the cross* (Philippians 2:8). This is not the cross in which Paul gloried, however. He would have shrunk with horror from the idea of glorying in a mere piece of wood. I have no doubt he would have denounced the Roman Catholic adoration of the crucifix as profane, blasphemous, and idolatrous.

The cross sometimes means the afflictions and trials which believers in Christ have to go through if they follow Christ faithfully for their religion's sake. This is the sense in which our Lord uses the word when He says, *he that does not take his cross and follow after me is not worthy of me* (Matthew 10:38; Luke 14:27). This also is not the sense in which Paul used the word when he wrote to the Galatians. He knew that cross well; he carried it patiently. But he is not speaking of it here.

But in some places the cross also indicates the doctrine that Christ died for sinners on the cross – the atonement that He made for sinners by His suffering for them on the cross, the complete and perfect sacrifice for sin that He offered when He gave His own body to be crucified. In short, this one word, the *cross*, stands for Christ crucified, the only Savior. This is the meaning in which Paul used the expression when he told the Corinthians *the word of the cross is foolishness to those that perish* (1 Corinthians 1:18). This is the meaning in which he wrote to the Galatians, *God forbid that I should glory, save in the cross.* He simply meant, "I glory in nothing but Christ crucified as the salvation of my soul."[2]

---

2   "By the cross of Christ the apostle understands the all-sufficient,

Reader, Jesus Christ crucified was the joy and the delight, the comfort and the peace, the hope and the confidence, the foundation and the resting place, the ark and the refuge, the food and the medicine of Paul's soul. He did not think of what he had done himself and suffered himself. He did not meditate on his own goodness and his own righteousness. He loved to think of what Christ had done and what Christ had suffered – of the death of Christ, the righteousness of Christ, the atonement of Christ, the blood of Christ, the finished work of Christ. In this he did glory. This was the sun of his soul.

This is the subject Paul *loved to preach about.* He proclaimed to sinners that the Son of God had shed His own heart's blood to save their souls. He walked up and down the world to tell people that Jesus Christ loved them and had died for their sins upon the cross. Take note of how he said to the Corinthians, *I delivered unto you first of all that which I also received, how that Christ died for our sins* (1 Corinthians 15:3). *I judged not to know anything among you, except Jesus Christ*

---

expiatory, and satisfactory sacrifice of Christ upon the cross, with the whole work of our redemption; in the saving knowledge of whereof, he professes he will glory and boasts." – Cudworth on Galatians, 1613. "Touching these words, I do not find that any expositor, either ancient or modern, Popish or Protestant, writing on this place, expounds the cross here mentioned of the sign of the cross, but of the profession of faith in Him that was hanged on the cross." – Mayer's Commentary, 1631.
"This is rather to be understood of the cross which Christ suffered for us than of that we suffer for Him" – Leigh's Annotations, 1650.

11

and him crucified (1 Corinthians 2:2). Paul, a blaspheming, persecuting Pharisee, had been washed in Christ's blood. He could not hold his peace about it. He was never weary of telling the story of the cross.

This is the subject he *loved to dwell upon when he wrote to believers.* It is wonderful to observe how full his epistles generally are of the sufferings and death of Christ and how they run over with "thoughts that breathe and words that burn"[3] about Christ's dying love and power. His heart seemed full of the subject. He enlarged on it constantly; he returned to it continually. It is the golden thread that runs through all his doctrinal teaching and practical exhortations. He seemed to think that the most advanced Christian could never hear too much about the cross.[4]

This is what he *lived* all his life from the time of his conversion. He told the Galatians, *The life which I now live in the flesh I live by the faith of the son of God, who loved me and gave himself for me* (Galatians 2:20). What made him so strong to labor? What made him so willing to work? What made him so unwearied in endeavoring to save some? What made him so persevering and

---

3   Thomas Gray

4   "Christ crucified is the sum of the gospel and contains all the riches of it. Paul was so taken with Christ that nothing sweeter than Jesus could drop from his pen and lips. It is observed that he wrote the word *Jesus* five hundred times in his epistles." – Charnock, from *The Works of the Late Rev. Stephen Charnock, B. D.*, 1684.

patient? I will tell you the secret. He was always feeding by faith on Christ's body and Christ's blood. Jesus crucified was the meat and drink of his soul.

And, you may rest assured that Paul was right. Depend upon the cross of Christ, the death of Christ on the cross to make atonement for sinners – that is the central truth in the whole Bible. This is the truth we begin with when we open Genesis. The seed of the woman bruising the serpent's head is nothing but a prophecy of Christ crucified. This is the truth that shines out, though veiled, all through the law of Moses and the history of the Jews. The daily sacrifice, the Passover lamb, the continual shedding of blood in the tabernacle and temple – all were emblems of Christ crucified.

This is the truth that we see honored in the vision of heaven before we close the book of Revelation. *in the midst of the throne and of the four animals*, we are told, *and in the midst of the elders, stood a Lamb as it had been slain* (Revelation 5:6). Even in the midst of heavenly glory we get a view of Christ crucified. Take away the cross of Christ, and the Bible is a dark book. It is like the Egyptian hieroglyphics without the key that interprets their meaning – curious and wonderful but of no real use.

Consider what I say. You may know a good deal about the Bible; you may know the outlines of the histories it contains and the dates of the events described, just as a man knows the history of England. You may know the names of the men and women mentioned in it, just as a man knows Caesar, Alexander the Great, or Napoleon. You may know several precepts of the Bible and admire them, just as a man admires Plato, Aristotle, or Seneca. But if you have not yet found out that Christ crucified is the foundation of the whole volume, you have read your Bible to very little profit. Your religion is a heaven without a sun, an arch without a keystone, a compass without a needle, a clock without spring or weights, or a lamp without oil. It will not comfort you. It will not deliver your soul from hell.

Consider what I say again. You may know a good deal about Christ with a kind of head knowledge. You may know who He was, where He was born, and what He did. You may know His miracles, His sayings, His prophecies, and His ordinances. You may know how He lived, how He suffered, and how He died. But unless you know the power of Christ's cross by experience, unless you know and feel within that the blood shed on that cross has washed away your own particular sins, and unless you are willing to confess that your salvation depends entirely on the work that Christ did upon the cross, Christ will profit you nothing. The mere knowing Christ's name will never save you. You must know His cross and His blood, or you will die in your sins.[5]

As long as you live, *beware of a religion in which little is said of the cross.* You live in times when this warning is sadly needful. Beware, I say again, of a religion without the cross.

Hundreds of places of worship exist today in which there is almost everything except the cross. There are carved oaks and sculptured stones; there are stained glass and brilliant paintings; there are solemn services and a constant round of ordinances, but the real cross of Christ is not there. Jesus crucified is not proclaimed in the pulpit. The Lamb of God is not lifted up, and salvation by faith in Him is not freely proclaimed. Therefore, all is wrong. Beware of such places of worship. They would not have satisfied the apostle Paul.[6]

Thousands of religious books are published today in which there is everything except the cross. They are full of directions about sacraments and praises of the

---

5   "If our faith stops in Christ's life and does not fasten upon His blood, it will not be justifying faith. His miracles, which prepared the world for His doctrines; His holiness, which fitted Himself for His sufferings, had been inefficient for us without being a fit addition of the cross." – Charnock, 1684.

6   "Paul determined to know nothing else but Jesus Christ and Him crucified. But many manage the ministry as if they had taken up a contrary determination – even to know anything except Jesus Christ and Him crucified." – Robert Traill, from *The Works of the Late Reverend Robert Traill, A.M.*, 1690.

church; they abound in exhortations about holy living and rules for the attainment of perfection; they have plenty of fonts and crosses both inside and outside, but the real cross of Christ is left out. The Savior and His dying love are either not mentioned or mentioned in an unscriptural way. Because of this they are worse than useless. Beware of such books. They would never have satisfied the apostle Paul.

Paul gloried in nothing but the cross. Strive to be like him. Set Jesus crucified fully before the eyes of your soul. Don't listen to any teaching that would place anything between you and Him. Don't fall into the old Galatian error; don't think that anyone is a better guide than the apostles. Don't be ashamed of the old paths in which men walked who were inspired by the Holy Spirit. Don't let the vague talk of men who speak great, swelling words about catholicity, the church, and the ministry disturb your peace and make you loosen your hands from the cross. Churches, ministers, and sacraments are all useful in their way, but they are not Christ crucified. Don't give Christ's honor to another. *He that glorieth, let him glory in the Lord.*

Why All Christians Should Glory in the Cross of Christ

I feel that I must say something on this point because of the ignorance that prevails about it. I suspect that many see no peculiar glory and beauty in the subject of Christ's cross. On the contrary, they think it painful, humbling, and degrading. They do not see much profit in the story of His death and sufferings. They'd rather turn from it as an unpleasant thing.

I believe that such persons are quite wrong. I cannot stand with them. I believe it is an excellent thing for us to be continually dwelling on the cross of Christ. It is a good thing to be reminded often of how Jesus was betrayed into the hands of wicked men, how they condemned Him with the most unjust judgment, how they spit on Him, scourged Him, beat Him, and crowned

Him with thorns, how they led Him forth as a lamb to the slaughter without His murmuring or resisting, how they drove the nails through His hands and feet and set Him up on Calvary between two thieves, and how they pierced His side with a spear, mocked Him in His suffering, and let Him hang there naked and bleeding until He died. Yes, it is good to be reminded of all these things.

It was not by accident that the crucifixion is described four times in the New Testament. There are very few things that all four writers of the Gospels describe. Generally speaking, if Matthew, Mark, and Luke tell a thing in our Lord's history, John does not tell it. But there is one thing that all four describe most fully, and that one thing is the story of the cross. This is a telling fact and not to be overlooked.

People seem to forget that all Christ's sufferings on the cross were *foreordained*. They did not come on Him by chance or accident; they were all planned, counseled, and determined from all eternity. The cross was foreseen in the provisions for the salvation of sinners. In the purposes of God, the cross was set up from everlasting. Not one throb of pain did Jesus feel, not one precious drop of blood did Jesus shed, which had not been appointed long ago. Infinite wisdom planned that redemption should be by the cross. Infinite wisdom brought Jesus to the cross in due time. He was crucified by the determinate counsel and foreknowledge of God.

People seem to forget that all Christ's sufferings on the cross were *only necessary for man's salvation.* He had to bear our sins, if they were ever to be borne at all. With His stripes alone could we be healed. This was the only payment of our debt that God would accept; this was the great sacrifice on which our eternal life depended. If Christ had not gone to the cross and suffered in our place, the just for the unjust, there would not have been a spark of hope for us. *For he has made him to be sin for us, who knew no sin, that we might be made the righteousness of God in him* (2 Corinthians 5:21). There would have been a mighty gulf between ourselves and God, which no man ever could have passed.[7]

People seem to forget that all Christ's sufferings were endured *voluntarily* and of His own free will. He was under no compulsion. Of His own choice He laid down His life; of His own choice He went to the cross to finish the work He came to do. He might easily have summoned legions of angels with a word and scattered Pilate and Herod and all their armies like chaff before the wind. But He was a willing sufferer. His heart was set on the salvation of sinners. He was resolved to open

---

7   "In Christ's humiliation stands our exaltation; in His weakness stands our strength; in His humiliation our glory; in His death our life." – Cudworth, 1618.

a fountain for all sin and uncleanness by shedding His own blood.

When I think of all this, I see nothing painful or disagreeable in the subject of Christ's cross. On the contrary, I see wisdom and power, peace and hope, joy and gladness, comfort and consolation. The more I keep the cross in my mind's eye, the more fullness I seem to discern in it. The longer I dwell on the cross in my thoughts, the more I am satisfied that there is more to be learned at the foot of the cross than anywhere else in the world.[8]

Can I know the length and breadth of *God the Father's love* towards a sinful world? Where would I see it most displayed? Shall I look at His glorious sun, shining down daily on the unthankful and evil? Shall I look at seedtime and harvest, returning in regular yearly succession?

I can find a stronger proof of love than anything of this sort. I look at the cross of Christ. I see in it not the cause of the Father's love, but the effect. *God increased the price of his charity toward us in that while we were yet sinners the Christ died for us* (Romans 5:8). There I see that God so loved this wicked world *that he gave*

---

8   "The eye of faith regards Christ sitting on the summit of the cross as in a triumphal chariot; the devil bound to the lowest part of the same cross and trodden under the feet of Christ." – Bishop Davenant, from *An Exposition of the Epistle of St. Paul to the Colossians*, 1627.

his only begotten Son – gave Him to suffer and die – *that whosoever believes in him should not perish but have eternal life* (John 3:16). I know that the Father loves us because He did not withhold His Son from us, His only Son.

I might sometimes fancy that God the Father is too high and holy to care for such miserable, corrupt creatures as we are! But I cannot, must not, dare not think it when I look at the cross of Christ.[9] Can I know how exceedingly *sinful and abominable sin is* in the sight of God? Where shall I see that most fully illustrated? Shall I turn to the history of the flood and read how sin drowned the world? Shall I go to the shore of the Dead Sea and note what sin did to Sodom and Gomorrah? Shall I turn to the wandering Jews and observe how sin has scattered them over the face of the earth? No, I can find still better proof.

I look at the cross of Christ. There I see that sin is so black and damnable that nothing but the blood of God's own Son can wash it away. There I see that sin has so separated me from my holy Maker that all the angels in heaven could never have made peace between

---

9   "The world we live in would have fallen upon our heads, had it not been upheld by the pillar of the cross; had Christ not stepped in and promised a satisfaction for the sin of man. By this all things consist – not a blessing we enjoy but may remind us of it; they were all forfeited by sin, but merited by His blood. If we study it well, we shall be sensible how God hated sin and loved a world." – Charnock.

us. Nothing could reconcile us short of the death of Christ. If I listened to the wretched talk of proud men, I might sometimes fancy that sin was not so very sinful. But I cannot think little of sin when I look at the cross of Christ.[10]

Can I know the *fullness and completeness of the salvation* God has provided for sinners? Where would I see it most distinctly? Shall I go to the general declarations in the Bible about God's mercy? Shall I rest in the general truth that God is a God of love? Oh no, I will look at the cross of Christ. I find no evidence like that. I find no balm for a sore conscience and a troubled heart like the sight of Jesus dying for me on the accursed tree. There I see that a full payment has been made for all my enormous debts. The curse of that law which I have broken has come down on One who suffered there in my place.

The demands of that law are all satisfied. Payment has been made for me, even to the uttermost farthing (equal to one-fourth of a British penny). It will not be required twice. I might sometimes imagine I was too bad to be forgiven; my own heart sometimes whispers that I am too wicked to be saved. But I know in my

---

10 "If God hates sin so much that He would allow neither man nor angel for the redemption thereof, but only the death of His only and well-beloved Son, who will not stand in fear?" – Church of England Homily for Good Friday, 1560.

better moments that this is all my foolish unbelief. I have an answer to my doubts in the blood shed on Calvary. I feel sure that there is a way to heaven for the very vilest of men, when I look at the cross.

Would I find strong *reasons for being a holy man*? Where shall I turn for them? Shall I only listen to the Ten Commandments? Shall I study the examples given in the Bible of what grace can do? Shall I meditate on the rewards of heaven and the punishments of hell? Is there no stronger motive than that?

Yes, I will look at the cross of Christ. There I see the love of Christ that constrains me to live not unto myself, but unto Him. There I see that I am not my own; I am bought with a price. As Paul told the Corinthians, *Ye are bought with a price, therefore glorify God in your body and in your spirit, which are God's* (1 Corinthians 6:20). I am bound by the most solemn obligations to glorify Jesus with body and spirit, which are His. At the cross I see that Jesus gave Himself for me, not only to redeem me from all iniquity, but also to purify me and make me one of a peculiar people, zealous of good works. He bore my sins in His own body on the tree so that I, being dead unto sin, should live unto righteousness. There is nothing so sanctifying as a clear view of the cross of Christ. It crucifies the world unto us, and us unto the world, for *those that are of the Christ have crucified the flesh with its affections and lusts. If we live by the Spirit, let us also walk in the Spirit* (Galatians 5:24-25). How can we love sin when we remember that because of our sins Jesus died? Surely, no one could be so holy as the disciples of a crucified Lord.

Could I learn *how to be contented and cheerful* under all the cares and anxieties of life? What school would I go to? How shall I attain this state of mind most easily? Shall I consider the sovereignty of God, the wisdom of God, the providence of God, the love of God? It is well to do so.

But I have a better argument. I will look at the cross of Christ. I feel that He who spared not His only begotten Son, but delivered Him up to die for me, will surely with Him give me all things that I need. He who endured that pain for my soul will surely not with-hold from me anything that is good. He who has done the greater things for me will doubtless do the lesser things also. He who gave His own blood to procure me a home will unquestionably supply me with all that is profitable for me along the way. There is no school for learning contentment than can be compared with the foot of the cross.

Can I gather *arguments for hoping that I shall never be cast away*? Where shall I go to find them? Shall I look at my own graces and gifts? Shall I take comfort in my own faith, and love, and penitence, and zeal, and prayer? Shall I turn to my own heart and say, "This same heart will never be false and cold"? Oh no! God forbid! I will look at the cross of Christ. This is my grand argument. This is my mainstay. I cannot think that He who went through such sufferings to redeem my soul will let that soul perish after it has once cast itself on Him. Oh no, what Jesus paid for, Jesus will surely keep, *therefore I am certain that neither death nor life nor angels nor principalities nor powers nor things present nor things to come nor height nor depth nor any creature shall be able to separate us from the charity of God, which is in Christ, Jesus our Lord* (Romans 8:38-39). He paid dearly for it. He will not let it be lost. He died for me when I was yet a dark sinner; He will never forsake me after I have believed. Ah, when Satan tempts you to doubt whether Christ's people will be kept from falling, you should tell Satan to look at the cross.[11]

And now, will you marvel that I said all Christians ought to glory in the cross? Don't you wonder that anyone can hear of the cross and remain unmoved? I declare I know no greater proof of man's depravity

---

11 "The believer is so freed from eternal wrath, that if Satan and conscience say, 'Thou art a sinner, and under the curse of the law,' he can say, 'It is true, I am a sinner; but I was hanged on a tree and died, and was made a curse in my Head and Lawgiver Christ, and his payment and suffering is my payment and suffering.'" – Samuel Rutherford, *Christ Dying and Drawing Sinners to Himself*, 1647.

than the fact that thousands of so-called Christians see nothing in the cross. Our hearts may be called stony, the eyes of our mind may be called blind, our whole nature may be called diseased, we may all be called dead when the cross of Christ is heard of but neglected. Surely, we may take up the words of the prophet and say, *Hear, O heavens, and give ear, O earth; a horrible and ugly thing is committed in the land* (Isaiah 1:2; Jeremiah 5:30). Christ was crucified for sinners, and yet many Christians live as if He was never crucified at all.

The cross is *the grand peculiarity of the Christian religion.* Other religions have laws and moral precepts, forms and ceremonies, rewards and punishments. But other religions cannot tell us of a dying Savior. They cannot show us the cross. This is the crown and glory of the gospel. This is that special comfort that belongs to it alone. Miserable indeed is that religious teaching which calls itself Christian but contains nothing of the cross. A man who teaches in this way might as well profess to explain the solar system but tell his hearers nothing about the sun.

The cross is *the strength of a minister.* I for one would not be without it for all the world. I would feel like a soldier without arms, an artist without his pencil, a pilot without his compass, or a laborer without his tools. Let others, if they desire, preach the law and morality; let others hold forth the terrors of hell and the joys of heaven; let others drench their congregations with teachings about the sacraments and the church, but give me the cross of Christ. This is the only lever that has ever turned the world upside down and made men forsake their sins. And if the preaching of the cross will not do this, nothing will.

A man may begin preaching with a perfect knowledge of Latin, Greek, and Hebrew, but he will do little or no good for his hearers unless he knows something of the cross. Never was there a minister who accomplished much for the conversion of souls who did not dwell on Christ crucified. Luther, Rutherford, Whitefield, and M'Cheyne were all outstanding preachers of the cross. The Holy Spirit delights to bless this preaching. He loves to honor those who honor the cross.

The cross is *the secret of the missionary success.* Nothing but this has ever moved the hearts of the heathen. As the cross has been lifted up, missions have prospered. This is the weapon that has won victories over hearts of every kind in every quarter of the globe: Greenlanders, Africans, South Sea Islanders, Hindus, and Chinese have all felt its power.

Just as that huge, iron tube which crosses the Menai Straits is more affected and bent by half an hour's sunshine than by all the dead weight that can be placed in it, so in like manner the hearts of savages have melted before the cross, when every other argument could move them no more than stones. "Brethren," said a North American Indian after his conversion, "I have been a heathen. I know how heathens think. Once a preacher came and began to explain to us that there was a God, but we told him to return to the place from whence he came. Another preacher came and told us not to lie, nor steal, nor drink, but we did not heed him. At last another came into my hut one day and said, 'I am come to you in the name of the Lord of heaven and earth to let you know that He will make you happy and deliver you from misery. For this end He became a man, gave His life a ransom, and shed His blood for sinners.' I could not forget his words. I told them to the other Indians, and an awakening began among us. I say, therefore, preach the sufferings and death of Christ our Savior if you wish your words to gain entrance among the heathen." Never indeed did the devil triumph so thoroughly as when he persuaded the Jesuit missionaries in China to keep back the story of the cross.

The cross is *the foundation of a church's prosperity.* No church will ever be honored in which Christ crucified is not continually lifted up; nothing whatever can make up for the lack of the cross. Without it all things may be done decently and in order; without it there may be splendid ceremonies, beautiful music, gorgeous churches, learned ministers, crowded communion tables, and huge collections for the poor; but without the cross no good will be done. Dark hearts will not be enlightened; proud hearts will not be humbled; mourning hearts will not be comforted, and fainting hearts will not be cheered.

Sermons about the Catholic Church and an apostolic ministry, sermons about baptism and the Lord's Supper, sermons about unity and schism, sermons about fasts and communion, and sermons about fathers and saints will never make up for the absence of sermons about the cross of Christ. They may amuse some, but they will feed none. A gorgeous banqueting room and splendid gold plate on the table will never satisfy a hungry man, for they lack food. Christ crucified is God's grand ordinance for good to men.

Whenever a church avoids Christ crucified or puts anything whatever in that foremost place that Christ crucified should always have, from that moment a church ceases to be useful. Without Christ crucified in her pulpits, a church is little better than a hindrance, a dead carcass, a well without water, a barren fig tree, a sleeping watchman, a silent trumpet, a dumb witness, an ambassador without terms of peace, a messenger without tidings, a lighthouse without fire, a stumbling block to weak believers, a comfort to infidels, a hotbed for formalism, a joy to the devil, and an offense to God.

The cross is *the grand center of union* among true Christians. Our outward differences are many, without doubt. One man is an Episcopalian, another is a Presbyterian; one is an Independent, another a Baptist; one is a Calvinist, another an Arminian; one is a Lutheran, another a Plymouth Brother; one is a friend to establishments, another a friend to the voluntary system; one is a friend to liturgies, another a friend to extemporary prayer. But in the end, what shall we hear in heaven about these differences? Nothing, most probably, nothing at all. *There is neither Jew nor Greek, there is neither slave nor free, there is neither male nor female; for ye are all one in Christ Jesus* (Galatians 3:28).

Does a man really and sincerely glory in the cross of Christ? That is the grand question. If he does, he is my brother; we are traveling on the same road; we are journeying towards a home where Christ is all, and everything outward in religion will be forgotten, *where there is neither Greek nor Jew, circumcision nor uncircumcision, Barbarian nor Scythian, slave nor free: but Christ is all, and in all* (Colossians 3:11). But if he does not glory in the cross of Christ, I cannot feel comfort about him. Union on outward points only is union only for a time; union about the cross is union for eternity. Error on outward points is only a skin-deep disease; error about the cross is disease at the heart. Union about outward points is a mere man-made union; union about the cross of Christ can only be produced by the Holy Spirit.

I don't know what you think of all this. I feel as if I have said nothing compared to what might be said. I feel as if the half of what I desire to tell you about the cross is left untold. But I do hope that I have given you something to think about. I do trust that I have shown you that I have reason for the question with which I began this little book: "What do you think and feel about the cross of Christ?" Consider now for a few moments how I apply the whole subject to your conscience.

Are you living in any kind of sin? Are you following the course of this world and neglecting your soul? Mark well what I say to you today: "Behold the cross of Christ." See there, at the cross, how Jesus loved you! See there what Jesus suffered to prepare a way of salvation for you.

Yes, careless men and women, for you that blood was shed. For you those hands and feet were pierced with nails. For you that body hung in agony on the cross. You are those whom Jesus loved and for whom

He died! Surely, that love ought to melt you. Surely, the thought of the cross should draw you to repentance.

Oh, that it might be so this very day. Oh, that you would come at once to that Savior who died for you and is willing to save you. Come, cry to Him with the prayer of faith, and I know that He will listen. Come, lay hold upon the cross, and I know that He will not cast you out. Come, believe on Him who died on the cross, and this very day you shall have eternal life. How will you ever escape if you neglect so great salvation (Hebrews 2:3)? None surely will be so deep in hell as those who despise the cross.

Are you inquiring about the way toward heaven? Are you seeking salvation but doubtful that you can find it? Are you desiring to have an interest in Christ but doubting that Christ will receive you? To you also I say, "Behold the cross of Christ." Here is encouragement if you really want it. Draw near to the Lord Jesus with boldness, for nothing needs to keep you back. His arms are open to receive you; His heart is full of love towards you. He has made a way by which you may approach Him with confidence. *Let us, therefore, come boldly unto the throne of his grace, that we may obtain mercy and find grace to help in time of need* (Hebrews 4:16). Think of the cross. Draw near, and fear not.

Are you an unlearned man? Are you desirous to get

to heaven but perplexed and brought to a standstill by difficulties in the Bible that you cannot explain? To you also I say, "Behold the cross of Christ." See there the Father's love and the Son's compassion. Surely, they are written in great, plain letters that none can mistake. Are you now perplexed by the doctrine of election? Can you not reconcile your own utter corruption and your own responsibility? Look at the cross. Doesn't that cross tell you that Jesus is a mighty, loving, ready Savior? Doesn't it make one thing plain – that if you are not saved, it is all your own fault? Oh, seize that truth and hold it fast!

Are you a distressed believer? Is your heart pressed down with sickness, tried with disappointments, over-burdened with cares? To you I say, "Behold the cross of Christ." Think of whose hand it is that chastens you; think of whose hand is measuring the cup of bitterness which you are drinking. It is the hand of Him who was crucified. That same hand was nailed to the accursed tree out of love for your soul. Surely, that thought should comfort and encourage you. Surely, you should say to yourself, "A crucified Savior will never lay upon me anything that is not good for me. There is a need; it must be well."

Are you a believer who longs to be more holy? Are you a person who finds his heart too ready to love earthly things? To you I say, "Behold the cross of Christ." Look at the cross; think of the cross; meditate on the cross, and then go and set your affections on the world if you can. I believe that holiness is nowhere learned so well as on Calvary; I believe you cannot look at the cross much without feeling your will sanctified and your tastes made more spiritual. As the sun that is gazed upon makes everything else look dark and dim, so the cross darkens the false splendor of this world. As honey makes all other things seem to have no taste at all, so the cross that is seen by faith takes all the sweetness out of the pleasures of the world. Continue every day steadily looking at the cross of Christ, and you will soon say of the world, as the poet does –

> Its pleasures now no longer please,
>> No more content afford;
> Far from my heart be joys like these,
>> Now I have seen the Lord.
>
> As by the light of opening day
>> The stars are all concealed;
> So earthly pleasures fade away,
>> When Jesus is revealed.[12]

---

12   John Newton, 1779.

Are you a dying believer? Have you gone to that bed from which something within tells you that you will never rise from it alive? Are you drawing near to that solemn hour when soul and body must part for a season and you must launch into a world unknown? Oh, look steadily at the cross of Christ, and you shall be kept in peace! Fix the eyes of your mind firmly on Jesus crucified, and He shall deliver you from all your fears. Though you walk through dark places, He will be with you. He will never leave you, never forsake you. Sit under the shadow of the cross to the very last, and its fruit shall be sweet to your taste. "Ah," said a dying missionary, "there is but one thing needful on a death-bed, and that is to feel one's arms around the cross!"

Reader, I lay these thoughts before your mind. What you think now about the cross of Christ, I cannot tell, but I can wish you nothing better than this – that you may be able to say with the apostle Paul before you die or meet the Lord, *God forbid that I should glory, save in the cross of our Lord Jesus Christ.*

J. C. Ryle – A Brief Biography

John Charles Ryle was born into a wealthy, affluent, socially elite family on May 10, 1816 – the first-born son of John Ryle, a banker, and his wife Susanna (Wirksworth) Ryle. As the firstborn, John lived a privileged life and was set to inherit all of his father's estate and pursue a career in Parliament. His future promised to be planned and comfortable with no material needs.

J. C. Ryle attended a private school and then earned academic scholarships to Eton (1828) and the University of Oxford (1834), but he excelled in sports. He particularly made his mark in rowing and cricket. Though his pursuit of sports was short lived, he claimed that they gave him leadership gifts. "It gave me a power of commanding, managing, organizing and directing, seeing through men's capabilities and using every man in the post to which he was best suited, bearing and forbearing, keeping men around me in good temper, which I have found of infinite use on lots of occasions in life, though in very different matters."

In 1837, before graduation, Ryle contracted a serious chest infection, which caused him to turn to the Bible and prayer for the first time in over fourteen years. One Sunday he entered church late as Ephesians 2:8 was being read – slowly, phrase by phrase. John felt the Lord was speaking to him personally, and he claims to have been converted at that moment through the Word without any commentary or sermon.

His biographer wrote, "He came under conviction, was converted, and from that moment to the last recorded syllable of this life, no doubt ever lingered in John's mind that the Word of God was living and powerful, sharper than any two-edged sword."

After graduation from Oxford, John went to London to study law for his career in politics, but in 1841, his father's bank crashed. That was the end of the career in politics, for he had no funding to continue.

In later years, John wrote, "We got up one summer's morning with all the world before us as usual, and went to bed that same night completely and entirely ruined. The immediate consequences were bitter and painful in the extreme, and humiliating to the utmost degree."

And at another time, he said, "The plain fact was there was no one of the family whom it touched more than it did me. My father and mother were no longer young and in the downhill of life; my brothers and sisters, of course, never expected to live at Henbury (the family home) and naturally never thought of it as their house after a certain time. I, on the contrary, as the eldest son, twenty-five, with all the world before me, lost everything, and saw the whole future of my life turned upside down and thrown into confusion."

After this financial ruin from abundance, Ryle was a commoner – all in a day. For the first time in his life, he needed a job. His education qualified him for the clergy, so with his Oxford degree, he was ordained and entered the ministry of the Church of England. He proceeded in a totally different direction with his first assignment in the ministry at Exbury in Hampshire, but it was a rural area riddled with disease. His recurring lung infection made a difficult couple of years until he was transferred to St. Thomas in Winchester. With his commanding presence, passionately held principles, and warm disposition, John's congregation grew so large and strong it needed different accommodations.

Ryle accepted a position at that time in Helmington, Suffolk, where he had much time to read theologians like Wesley, Bunyan, Knox, Calvin, and Luther. He was a contemporary of Charles Spurgeon, Dwight Moody, George Mueller, and Hudson Taylor. He lived in the age of Dickens, Darwin, and the American Civil War. All of these influenced Ryle's understanding and theology.

His writing career began from the tragedy of the Great Yarmouth suspension bridge. On May 9, 1845, a large crowd gathered for the official grand opening festivities, but the bridge collapsed and more than a hundred people plunged into the water and drowned. The incident shocked the whole country but it led Ryle to write his first tract. He spoke of life's uncertainties and God's sure provision of salvation through Jesus Christ. Thousands of copies were sold.

That same year, he married Matilda Plumptre, but she died after only two years, leaving him with an infant daughter. In 1850, he married Jessie Walker, but she had a lingering sickness, which caused Ryle to care for her and their growing family (three sons and another daughter) for ten years until she died. In 1861, he was transferred to Stradbroke, Suffolk, where he married Henrietta Clowes.

Stradbroke, Suffolk, was Ryle's last parish, and he gained a reputation for his straightforward preaching and evangelism. Besides his travelling and preaching, he spent time writing. He wrote more than 300 pamphlets, tracts, and books. His books include *Expository Thoughts on the Gospels* (7 Volumes, 1856-1869), *Principles for Churchmen* (1884), *Home Truths, Knots Untied, Old Paths,* and *Holiness.*

His *Christian Leaders of the Eighteenth Century* (1869) is described as having "short, pithy sentences, compelling logic and penetrating insight into spiritual power." This seems to be the case with most of his writing as he preached and wrote with five main guidelines: (1) Have a clear view of the subject, (2) Use simple words, (3) Use a simple style of composition, (4) Be direct, and (5) Use plenty of anecdotes and illustrations.

In all of his success with writing, he used the royalties to pay his father's debts. He may have felt indebted to that financial ruin, for he said, "I have not the least doubts, it was all for the best. If I had not been ruined, I should never have been a clergyman, never preached a sermon, or written a tract or book."

In spite of all of the trials that Ryle experienced – financial ruin, loss of three wives, his own poor health – he learned several life lessons. First, care and tend to your own family. Second, swim against the tide when you need to. He was evangelical before it was popular and he held to principles of Scripture: justification by faith alone, substitutionary atonement, the Trinity, and preaching. Third, model Christian attitudes toward your opponents. Fourth, learn and understand church history. Important benefits come from past generations. Fifth, serve in old age; "die in the harness." And, sixth, persevere through your trials.

These were life principles that Ryle learned as he lived his life, as he preached, as he wrote, and as he spread the gospel. He was forever a supporter of evangelism and a critic of ritualism.

J. C. Ryle was recommended by Prime Minister Benjamin Disraeli to be Bishop of Liverpool in 1880 where he then worked to build churches and mission halls to reach the whole city. He retired in 1900 at the age of 83 and died later that year. His successor described him as "a man of granite with a heart of a child."

G. C. B. Davies said "a commanding presence and fearless advocacy of his principles were combined with a kind and understanding attitude in his personal relationships."

Sources:

William P. Farley, "J. C. Ryle: A 19th-century Evangelical," *Enrichment Journal, http://enrichmentjournal.ag.org/200604/200604_120_jcryle.cfm.*

"J. C. Ryle," *The Banner of Truth, https://banneroftruth.org/us/about/banner-authors/j-c-ryle/.*

"J. C. Ryle," *Theopedia, https://www.theopedia.com/john-charles-ryle.*

David Holloway, "J. C. Ryle – The Man, The Minister and The Missionary," *Bible Bulletin Board, http://www.biblebb.com/files/ryle/j_c_ryle.htm.*

Other Similar Titles

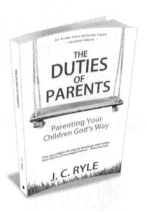

The Duties of Parents, by J. C. Ryle

In *The Duties of Parents*, J. C. Ryle presents seventeen simple and yet profound responsibilities of Christian parents. Nothing new is contained in this little volume, yet what is presented has the potential to change future generations both now and for eternity. Learn how to shepherd your children; learn how to utilize the most significant key of all – love; and learn first and foremost how to present and represent Christ to your children. As you read this book, expect to find yourself both challenged and excited to begin a wonderful, appropriate, and growing relationship with the most wonderful gift God can give us in our lifetime – our dear children.

Available where books are sold.

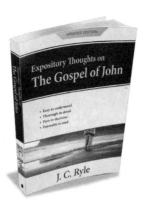

Expository Thoughts on the Gospel of John, by J. C. Ryle

Wisdom, encouragement, and exhortation is contained in these pages. Not because of the author's brilliance, but because of the words of truth contained in the gospel of John. And just as the Apostle John didn't draw any attention to himself, so also J. C. Ryle clearly and wonderfully directs his words and our thoughts towards the inspired words of scripture. If we truly love God, we will love His word; and the more study His word, the more we will love God.

Available where books are sold.

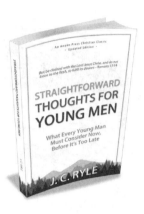

Straightforward Thoughts for Young Men,
by J. C. Ryle

Young men, you form a large and very important class in the population of this country; but where, and in what condition, are your souls? I am growing old myself, but there are few things that I can remember so well as the days of my youth. I have a most distinct recollection of the joys and the sorrows, the hopes and the fears, the temptations and the difficulties, the mistaken judgments and the misplaced affections, and the errors and the aspirations which surround and accompany a young man's life. If I can only say something to keep some young man walking in the right way and preserve him from faults and sins, which may hurt his prospects both for time and eternity, I shall be very thankful.

Available where books are sold.

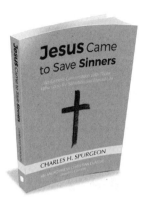

Jesus Came to Save Sinners,
by Charles H. Spurgeon

This is a heart-level conversation with you, the reader. Every excuse, reason, and roadblock for not coming to Christ is examined and duly dealt with. If you think you may be too bad, or if perhaps you really are bad and you sin either openly or behind closed doors, you will discover that life in Christ is for you too. You can reject the message of salvation by faith, or you can choose to live a life of sin after professing faith in Christ, but you cannot change the truth as it is, either for yourself or for others. As such, it behooves you and your family to embrace truth, claim it for your own, and be genuinely set free for now and eternity. Come and embrace this free gift of God, and live a victorious life for Him.

Available where books are sold.

Words of Warning,
by Charles H. Spurgeon

This book, *Words of Warning,* is an analysis of people and the gospel of Christ. Under inspiration of the Holy Spirit, Charles H. Spurgeon sheds light on the many ways people may refuse to come to Christ, but he also shines a brilliant light on how we can be saved. Unsaved or wavering individuals will be convicted, and if they allow it, they will be led to Christ. Sincere Christians will be happy and blessed as they consider the great salvation with which they have been saved.

Available where books are sold.

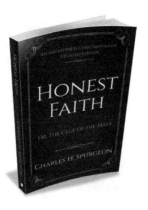

Honest Faith, by Charles H. Spurgeon

The paragraphs of this little book are not supposed to be an argument. It was not my aim to convince an opponent but to assist a friend. How I have personally threaded the labyrinth of life thus far may be of helpful interest to some other soul who is in a maze. I hope that these pages will assist some true heart to say "he fought his doubts and gather'd strength." Let no man's heart fail him, for the prevalent skepticisms of today are but "spectres of the mind." Face them, and they fly.

Available where books are sold.

According to Promise,
by Charles H. Spurgeon

The first part of this book is meant to be a sieve to separate the chaff from the wheat. Use it on your own soul. It may be the most profitable and beneficial work you have ever done. He who looked into his accounts and found that his business was losing money was saved from bankruptcy.

The second part of this book examines God's promises to His children. The promises of God not only exceed all precedent, but they also exceed all imitation. No one has been able to compete with God in the language of liberality. The promises of God are as much above all other promises as the heavens are above the earth.

Available where books are sold.

Following Christ, by Charles H. Spurgeon

You cannot have Christ if you will not serve Him. If you take Christ, you must take Him in all His qualities. You must not simply take Him as a Friend, but you must also take Him as your Master. If you are to become His disciple, you must also become His servant. God-forbid that anyone fights against that truth. It is certainly one of our greatest delights on earth to serve our Lord, and this is to be our joyful vocation even in heaven itself: *His servants shall serve Him: and they shall see His face* (Revelation 22:3-4).

Available where books are sold.

The Overcoming Life,
by Dwight L. Moody

Are you an overcomer? Or, are you plagued by little sins that easily beset you? Even worse, are you failing in your Christian walk, but refuse to admit and address it? No Christian can afford to dismiss the call to be an overcomer. The earthly cost is minor; the eternal reward is beyond measure.

Available where books are sold.